One Came Back

One Came Back

The Memoirs of Edwin L. Slagle

Compiled by
Maureen D. Slagle

VANTAGE PRESS
New York

FIRST EDITION

All rights reserved, including the right of
reproduction in whole or in part in any form.

Copyright © 2006 by Maureen D. Slagle

Published by Vantage Press, Inc.
419 Park Ave. South, New York, NY 10016

Manufactured in the United States of America
ISBN: 0-533-15292-5

Library of Congress Catalog Card No.: 2005906424

0 9 8 7 6 5 4 3 2 1

Author's Note

These are the memoirs written by my husband, Edwin L. Slagle, based on his wartime experiences as a fighter pilot during World War II. I have compiled and collated these into the present collection.

One Came Back

The day they attacked Pearl Harbor I volunteered at the Air Force Recruiting Office in Cleveland. I was sent to Keeslar Field, Mississippi. There, after processing, recruits were sent to SAACC (San Antonio Aviation Cadet Center) for further testing and classifying. Testing was rigorous—both mental and physical. I was one of the roughly 10 percent approved for pilot training and promoted from the rank of private to that of cadet. Two medics (sergeants in rank) rejected me because I had lost about one-third of my right thigh in a hunting accident some years earlier. I wanted to appeal but there was no higher ranked individual in the testing facility that day. I returned the next day and went to the office of the colonel in charge of the testing facilities and asked his clerk for an appointment. I met with the colonel who was both sympathetic and interested. He told me to meet him at the testing laboratory at 9 A.M. the next day. At the lab he asked me to lie on my back on an examining table. He took hold of my right foot and asked me to pull as hard as I could. He landed on top of me. Then he said, "Bend your right leg with your knee close to your shoulder." Again he took hold of my right foot and told me to push as hard as I could. He fell onto his back on an examining table across the aisle. Glaring at the two sergeants he said sarcastically, "This man can fly."

From SAACC I was sent to Coleman Field, Texas, for primary training in PT-19s, Fairchild Primary Trainers—low wing, single-engine monoplanes. After completing primary training successfully, I was sent to Perrin Field, Texas, for basic training in BT-13s (referred to at that time as Vultee Vibrators because of the shudder which occurred at stall speed). After completing basic training, I was sent to Foster Field, Texas for advanced training in the AT-6 North American Texan—a low wing, high performance plane and for training in the P-40 (single-engine fighter aircraft). I graduated on August 4, 1944, from Foster Field with the rank of 2nd Lieutenant and rating of Pilot, Single Engine (MOS 1090).

Thinking that I would receive P-38 training (P-38s were equipped with radar) I volunteered for radar training. In the armed services it is conventional wisdom that volunteering is not a good idea. Sure enough, I found myself trained in navigation using dead reckoning and in the use of the Norden bombsight at Victorville, California. After that things went from bad to worse, I was sent to Langley Field, Virginia, where I was taught to perform these functions using radar. This training resulted in the rating of Radar Bombardier/Navigator (MOS 0142) in addition to my pilot rating of MOS 1090.

Thus I arrived at North Field, Guam, one of five individuals with a rating of MOS 0142. We climbed out of a jeep, trudged up a hill and reported to Colonel Meany. I saluted. He said: "We don't bother with that here. Why is someone wearing pilot's wings flying a radar set?" I said: "It's a long story and I tend to cry a lot when I tell it." He laughed and said, "I'll take care of it. I'll set matters straight but not immediately because I've been on the phone to Washington every day for five weeks pressing for twenty-five Radar B/Ns, and, having finally received five, I'm in no position to immediately use one as a pilot." He told me to be patient while he worked it out; he did. To even be assigned for B-29 pilot training back in the States required 2,000 hours of multi-engine pilot time. I had zero.

So I became, probably, the first and only pilot with zero multi-engine hours to fly a B-29. By the book, it required 2,000 multi-engine hours of pilot time. The colonel had a major give me a B-29 check ride, and I was given the rating of B-29 Pilot. A second check ride resulted in my rating of B-29 Airplane Commander. I have often wondered if the major knew that I had never before had my hands on the controls of a B-29. The colonel knew it.

When I first reported for duty on Guam, Colonel Meany had said that because of the pressure he had put on Washington for Radar B/Ns, he could not immediately put me in the front seat, but that it would get done. For eleven missions I flew as the Radar B/N. This involved working with the navigator to ensure that, in flying over 3,000 to 4,000 miles of Pacific Ocean we did not wind up in the wrong place—e.g. the ocean. It also involved, when flying at night, or over cloud cover, dropping the bombs by radar. Night or day, if we were flying at an altitude within reach of anti-aircraft batteries, the Radar B/N had the job of confusing anti-aircraft batteries usually operated by radar. Radar controlled guns could "see" through cloud cover and were more accurate than those under human control. Confusing the radar involved standing in the rear of the plane near an open outside door located behind the back capsule on the right side of the plane. From this position I threw out of the door rather large, heavy rolls of tinfoil. As the rolls hit the slipstream they would unroll and flutter behind us. Enemy radar would be confused and direct some of its fire at the tinfoil. I also threw out of the door packets of tinfoil sheets, which would hit the slipstream, break open, and flutter behind us. Enemy anti-aircraft guns shot down a lot of tinfoil and, occasionally, a B-29.

I had taken advanced single-engine (fighter pilot) training at Foster Field, Texas. It was a rather large field with six training centers consisting of six one-storied buildings. Lt. Adamson was commanding officer for our squadron. Each center had five or six training officers (lieutenants) with three students to train. My trainer was an excellent pilot and trainer and friendly young man. He was killed by a student pilot before we completed our training. This happened at an auxiliary field—each large training field having auxiliary fields complete with a one-man control tower to relieve the congestion at the main field.

The landing flight pattern was standard at all airfields. My trainer was turning onto the approach leg of the pattern, preparing to land. As he turned, he saw that he was about to collide with another plane coming in from a right-hand pattern. He did the only thing he could do—hit the power. Because of his reduced speed, his plane rolled left due to engine torque, dived, and crashed. He was killed. The student pilot flying that plane should have spent the rest of his life peeling potatoes.

Student pilots were required to practice landings (called "shooting" landings) at an auxiliary field located near the main base. These fields relieved congestion at the main base. I was assigned to practice landings at such a field on a day when the wind was very strong, an estimated 45 mph with gusts making things very dicey. Preparing to take off I followed the standard procedure of parking near the end of the runway from which I would initiate my take-off to check the left and right magnetos. If there was a drop of 125 rpm, or more, on either magneto, the order was not to take off. Suddenly I was hit by a very strong gust, which spun the plane around. I hit the brakes and the plane went tail up wrecking the propeller, which, of course, damaged the engine. After I had contacted Foster Field by radio and reported the situation, Adamson, arrived. "You have big feet," he said.

A trainee who damaged a plane was required to appear before the "Board." This usually meant goodbye flying career. First, though, came a check ride by another instructor. Adamson elected to personally give me the check ride which consisted of every aerobatic in the book, plus out-of-control spins left, right, tight, and flat. After the ride he got out of the plane without a word and went into the squad room. I learned when I entered and joined my instructor and two other students that he had told my instructor that it was the best check ride he had ever given. Then I went into his office and was given a report form to fill out. The top portion of the form called for a description of the accident. I filled it out. The bottom half of the form asked how the accident could have been avoided. I suggested that all trainees be given training in ground control. Adamson hit the ceiling, but I refused to change my comments. He jumped up, red in the face, and issued me a "direct order" to make the change. I refused. I had never seen anyone quite that angry. The form was sent to the Board and I spent a sleepless night thinking that my flying career was over. The next day when I reported to my instructor, he was wearing a big grin and told me that by order of the Board, and effective immediately, all trainees were to be given four hours of ground control training and that I did not have to appear before the Board.

Upon successful completion of training in bombing and navigation using radar, I was one of five flying officers from Langley Field, Virginia, traveling west by train with orders specifying a destination having an APO 13 (Army

Post Office) number. This meant nothing to us or to command centers we arrived at on our way to our ultimate destination, Guam. At Hamilton Field, California, we reported to the command center. They didn't know what to do with us. We spent five days there and then received orders, which took us to Honolulu. Same situation there—they couldn't tell from our orders just what they were supposed to do with us. We spent another five days and were put on a plane, which took us to Johnson Field, Guam. At Johnson Field it was the same story and they held us there. There were no facilities there to house or feed us so we slept on tables in a nearby unused mess hall. We ate very well catching a ride to a Navy Pier near Agana and standing out on the pier facing an aircraft carrier docked at an adjacent pier. A motor launch would come to the pier from the carrier and one of the Navy enlisted men on board would ask if we would like to see over the carrier. We always arrived at mealtime. We would accept the invitation and enjoy the great food—no Spam, dehydrated potatoes and eggs, etc. We ate steak (cooked to order), real potatoes, fresh baked bread, hot apple pie *a la mode*, etc. They had a bakery on board and made their own ice cream. Thought at the time that if another war came along, I would join the Navy.

It took another five days to sort things out. At long last we arrived at North Field, Guam. Of the five of us only one came back, me. Three were killed and one became, to the best of my knowledge, a section eight (a mental case). I was probably a section eight but didn't know it. Another thing we didn't know at the time was that all the misrouting, mistakes, and just plain bumbling would eventually lead to dropping bombs on Japan.

A Guam-to-Japan round trip took twelve to eighteen hours. The reason our marines took Iwo Jima was to provide a place for B-29s to land in case of damage or fuel shortage.

Japanese lived on Iwo, even after we had taken it. They had a hospital, sleeping quarters, and mess hall underground. They would come out at night and do close order drill on the runway. Iwo had no facilities, no buildings, and no food except for the C-rations available courtesy of the marines stationed there. One night we were sleeping in our plane, parked just off the runway, when we were awakened by the bright light of a star flare set off by Japanese who had stumbled over a trip wire. The bright light was followed by machine gun fire. In the morning we found seven dead Japanese soldiers under or near our plane.

There were many dead Japanese within sight of the runway. I would see them as I walked along the runway during daylight hours. One day I sat down next to one and took his billfold out of his pocket which held many pieces of Japanese currency. I took one bill as a souvenir. In the billfold I also found a snapshot of his wife and small daughter. I did not like the way it made me feel.

At both ends of the runway were machine gun nests manned by our marines. Whenever we were on Iwo I would visit with the marines. Once while walking the runway a Seabee driving a truck gave me a lift. He asked me to take off my hat. It was an officer's hat and it had a rather large brass emblem on the front above the visor. I took it off and asked why. He pointed out that there was considerable enemy rifle fire directed at us. I had been aware of it while walking the runway and visiting the marine machine gun nests. I remarked that the Japanese were obviously lousy shots. He laughed and said, "They always shoot at anyone wearing brass and they might hit me instead of you."

After graduating at Foster Field, I did something that no one in the armed services is ever supposed to do, I volunteered. It wasn't the smartest move I ever made and I lived to regret it. A notice on the bulletin board called for volunteers for radar training. With visions of flying that hot twin boom P-38 Lightning fighter which was radar equipped, I was suckered in. I had lots of company. We lived to regret the stupid decision to, of all things, volunteer. We wound up with a rating of MOS1042-Radar Bombardier/Navigator, sitting in the rear of multi-engine aircraft at a radar set, and trained to use the set to navigate and bomb. Sad state of affairs for a single-engine fighter pilot, but all's well that ends well.

The colonel assigned me to the position of mission controller (one on each shift) and suggested that I fly missions acting as pilot observer to get the hang of things. After two or three missions, I was given a check ride and then a B-29 pilot rating. Then another check ride and given the rating of airplane commander. After that I flew with any crew which needed a pilot. That is how I became the only single-engine pilot (650 single-engine hours) with zero multi-engine time to fly a B-29. I doubt that the major who gave me the check ride knew that I had multi-engine hours. The colonel knew it.

The crews manning B-29s in the Marianas were trained at Wichita, Kansas, where the planes were produced. After training, the crews flew the planes to the Mariana Islands (Guam, Saipan, or Tinian) and then flew combat missions to Japan. Due to crew losses replacement personnel were needed. With a replacement group of five individuals I had arrived on Guam assigned to the 19th Bomb Group of the 20th Air Force. With the group was my friend, Tom Marshall, of Bakersfield, California. We had met at Langley Field, Virginia, while we were undergoing training in the use of radar to navigate and bomb. We buddied up and spent a lot of time together. Upon completion of the program we were told that radar operators were needed in both the European and Pacific theaters of war and that we had a choice. His home being in California, Tom urged me to join him in choosing the Pacific theater because he was most anxious for this mid-westerner to see California. It was not a hard sell. I had never been west of the Mississippi and was delighted to head that way with a dear friend. Thus, after a cross-country trip on a troop train, we arrived early one morning at a dock on the east side of San Francisco Bay and south of the Oakland-San Francisco Bay Bridge, in Oakland, California. We boarded a ferry, which took us to the San Francisco Ferry Building. Standing together on the bow, we watched the sun's rays coming up over the Oakland hills and coming slowly down over San Francisco lighting up the hilltops located between the city and the Pacific Ocean. As the sun rose, the rays descended from the hilltops to finally blanket the city from the hilltops to the docks aligning the Bay Shore. The sheer beauty of the scene unfolding before my eyes transfixed me.

Tom said, "Well, what do you think?" I replied, "If I get out of the war alive. I will live in California." I did get out alive. Tom did not. I lived for many years near San Francisco—initially in nearby Pittsburg because I was employed there by U.S. Steel. I had transferred there from a U.S. Steel plant in Cleveland where I had been employed before the war.

Tom said that, sooner or later, he would not be back because his crew was fouled up. "Sooner, or later, I probably won't be returning from a mission," Tom had said, "my crew is all fouled up." He was right. His plane went down over Tokyo on the night of May 24, 1945. I was so upset by this loss that, although not scheduled, I volunteered for, and flew, a mission over Tokyo the next night.

Richard Saleeby, also one of the five, was lost on a night raid. The weather was poor—heavy rain and high winds.

His plane lost three engines between Guam and Iwo—a distance of about 600 miles. The crew bailed out at 2,000 feet about 20 miles south of Iwo Jima. I located nine of them. They were in life rafts and using flashlights to attract our attention. We had been flying past Iwo. I had the radio tuned to Ranger (Iwo) tower and volunteered to search. Ranger told me that they could use some help and that all that they could do was send out a destroyer which had no hope of finding life rafts at night in a storm. I spotted a flickering flashlight, notified Ranger tower, circled the spot, and instructed the radioman to shoot off flares at 30-second intervals. The destroyer picked up the nine. Saleeby was not one of them. I stayed on the search pattern until after daylight and we were low on fuel.

I am not sure what happened to Gene Mason. He appeared to have mental or nerve problems. The last time I saw him he was sitting on the edge of his cot and throwing his trench knife point into the floor over and over and over again.

Dick Jones of Minden, Nevada, was killed in a landing accident during a daylight training flight at North Field.

One day, while on Guam, I walked past the command Quonset hut and heard behind me the Quonset door slam open and footsteps running in my direction. A voice called out, "Eddie!" I turned around and found myself in a near embrace with Adamson. Suddenly we were long-lost bosom buddies. From that day on he came to my Quonset every day. He wanted advice about his relationships with his parents, girlfriend, and crew. He came to me one day and said that his pilot (Adamson was an airplane commander) had refused to fly with him on a mission scheduled for later that day. Because I was at that time twenty-seven years old and most crew members were less than twenty, I was called "Pop" and was often called upon to help with personal problems. Adamson told me that he thought he should report this refusal to the command center. I told him that an investigation would include the interrogation of all his crew members from which it would be concluded that he was suffering from a superiority complex, was hated by his crew members, and was best described as insufferable. His flying career could well come to an abrupt halt. "Keep your mouth shut," I told him, "I'll fly in place of your pilot." Thus I have one mission more than will be found in official records.

One evening late, while I was still in the training command, I was trying to go to sleep, but a few feet away, sitting around a table, was a group of aviation cadets arguing about spin recovery. The argument centered on the NACA (National Aeronautics Committee Administration) spin recovery procedure—i.e., to recover from a spin, place the controls with the spin (stick in lap to the left for a left spin, or right for a right spin, rudder left for a left spin; right for a right spin). After about three revolutions, a slight shudder should be felt (the fuselage is churning up the slipstream but after about three revolutions, settles down into a pattern which sends a bit of slipstream over the airfoils, rudder, elevators and ailerons). The slipstream over the control surfaces causes the slight shudder. If the pilot acts quickly to put the stick straight forward and to kick full opposite rudder, the plane will recover and go into a dive. After flying speed is reached the plane is fully maneuverable. Some of the group took the position that the three-revolution procedure was ineffective because after that a recovery was not possible—some disagreed and a heated debate was in progress. Knowing that it was going to be a long night if I didn't stop the argument, I grabbed my hat, put it upside down on the table, and announced that anyone who thought that a spin was unbreakable after three revolutions should put his money where his mouth was. I covered all bets and announced that the next day I would spin in excess of three revolutions and break the spin. They, collectively, put fifty dollars in the hat and selected a pilot to go up in his own plane to act as observer. I covered the bets.

We went up the next day as planned. I took my AT6 as high as it would go, (called the plane's service ceiling, 16,000 feet) and put the plane into a spin. After six revolutions I put the controls into the NACA recovery position and waited for a shudder so I could break the spin. There was no shudder. Tried a recovery. Nothing. Placed the controls with the spin again. The NACA recovery failed again. I kept my eyes on the altimeter and learned that I was losing 500 feet of altitude per revolution. Tried waiting four or five revolutions. Nothing. Repeated the process three or four times. Nothing. Unbuckled my seatbelt and started over the side. Thought about the fifty dollars—that and pure stubbornness prevailed. This time I put in the NACA recovery and decided to ride it out—i.e., wait for the shudder rather than trying to recover without it. At 2,000 feet I nearly bailed out but sat back down, rebuckled my seat belt, and waited. The ground and trees were getting much too close for comfort. Suddenly I felt a shudder. I can't possibly describe the feeling of relief. The NACA recovery worked, as it should. Of course you knew that, otherwise, I wouldn't be around to talk about it. After landing, I checked the bottom of the plane and found green stains and leaves there.

Whenever I returned from a mission, I dropped to the ground from the nose wheel well and joined the repair crew chief in a visual inspection of the wings, wheels, controls, and fuselage. During the walk-around I would fill him in on any problems with the plane I'd noted during the mission. It was the repair crew's responsibility to put the plane back in

A-1 condition prior to the next flight. After one such inspection we were standing near the side of the plane looking at it. Our plane had encountered heavy flak from the Japanese anti-aircraft batteries. The repair crew chief said, "It looks like a piece of Swiss cheese," and asked, "What are you thinking?" I replied, "There must be a better way to make a living."

The Japanese knew where to place their guns. Japan is in the Northern hemisphere where the winds are called "the prevailing westerlies." Bomb runs were always made headed into the wind because that lowers ground speed, thereby increasing accuracy. The aircraft batteries were located along a line extending eastward to the coastline from all cities of any consequence. The batteries were mobile and would be relocated if necessary due to a change in wind direction. Bombing from any direction than into the wind had a negative impact on accuracy.

From our Quonset hut there was a line of Quonsets housing various operations—weather, communications, etc. In front of operations a jeep was parked most of the time and we often saw a colonel use the jeep. He was the West Point type: everything highly polished including his leather leggings and brass— and his uniform was always cleaned and pressed. Aircrews wore fatigues, green leather, and green brass. Brass and leather turned green with mold in a very short time—jungle and high humidity go hand in hand. The day after Japan ceased resistance because the United States had dropped the second atom bomb, we had a visit from the colonel. It was mid-morning and aircrews usually slept in late. This habit had its origin in the fact that we frequently came back from our missions at about daybreak.

One day I was awakened by a sergeant, calling orders.

"Hut, two, three, four. Hut, two, three, four." There was a clicking of heels. Someone marched up the two or three steps to the door of our hut, slammed the door open and shouted the command "Ten hut!" I raised my head to take a look. The sergeant was holding the door open as the polished colonel marched smartly up the steps and came to a halt with a loud click of his heels. Again the sergeant barked, "Ten hut!" I was three or four row of cots from the door. Luke, a pilot, had his cot nearest the door. Luke raised his head and said, "Something we can do for you, colonel?" The colonel saw nothing but aircrew members lying in their bunks with absolutely no intention of stirring. His dream of turning the airfield combat crews into a stateside-type training center was shattered. He beat a hasty retreat. It was clear that he did not have the support of the field commander.

I was the only one on the field with dry clothes and books , brass not corroded, and with clean, dry shoes. To arrange for this I had "requisitioned" lumber, tools, screws, nails, wire, tape, etc. and built a cupboard and an upright closet. These kept my clothes, books, and shoes warm and dry because each cupboard had a lighted light bulb in it. Our Quonsets had no electricity, but I solved that problem by running a wire out to a power line, which ran along the so-called road. All I had to do was climb a power pole and tap into the power line—taking care to avoid electrocution.

The war was over after the U.S. dropped two atom bombs—one on Hiroshima and one on Nagasaki in August of 1945. On September 5, 1945, a formation consisting of a large number of B-29s circled over the battleship *Missouri* which was anchored in Tokyo Bay. On the deck General MacArthur and Japanese officials signed the terms of the Japanese surrender. I was the pilot of one of those planes. After the signing, we flew a show of strength mission along the 38th parallel putting North Korea on notice that, if they messed up, their landscape would resemble Tokyo's. The last flight I took was returning a B-29 from Guam to Mather Field, California. We stopped at Kwajalein, an atoll in the Marshall Islands, between Guam and Hawaii. It was a rest and refueling area for planes. We were met by an air force officer who drove up to our plane in a jeep as we rolled to a stop after landing. We followed him and parked the plane as directed. He showed us to a Quonset hut where we could rest overnight. He then pointed to a nearby Quonset and told us that it was a mess hall and that they would take good care of us. We asked him if bacon and eggs were a possibility. On Guam we had had only dehydrated eggs and potatoes and only Spam for meat. He said that the mess hall did have bacon, eggs, and real potatoes and that the mess sergeant would take good care of us. It didn't happen that way. The mess sergeant was rude and served the routine, god-awful chow. Disappointed, we returned to our quarters. A short time later someone looked out of a window and called out, "The mess hall's on fire!" We rushed over to the burning mess hall to watch. It was totally destroyed. As we watched, I looked at the person standing next to me. It was the rude mess sergeant. When he looked at me, I said, "Next time a combat crew asks for something other than your routine chow, I suggest that you treat them and their request with a little more respect." His jaw dropped open and I bet that for a long time he wondered just how the fire started.

Dick Jones, a navigator, was with his crew and they were slow timing (a term used when a new engine was being broken in on a four-hour flight in which the new engine was operated at something less than cruising rpm). Upon landing, the plane took a bad bounce, not really unusual, especially in a crosswind, or if the wind was gusty. It is impossible to fly a lot and not experience a bad bounce now and then. The pilot tried to recover by hitting the throttles to regain flying speed. That was a fatal mistake. At a speed less than flying speed and in such a recovery attempt, one must be very careful with the throttle. Too much, and the plane does two things—gains maybe a few feet of altitude and rolls left due to engine torque. Left wing catches the ground. Taps for some or all on board. This is what happened to Dick and the entire crew except for the tail gunner who suffered a severe head injury. I later heard that he was out of his mind and raving mad.

Next day, there was an announcement over the PA system, "All pilots report to the briefing tent." It was a large tent set up auditorium style. General Curtis Lemay walked briskly into the tent, up the aisle to the stage and took the microphone as we all stood at attention. He issued an order. To the best of my memory it was, "If you take a bad bounce while landing, push on the stick, hold it there. Keep the plane down. You may take some fatalities but some of the crew will walk away." He walked back down the aisle and out of the tent.

Most aircrews regarded a mission as "all in a day's work." Read, ate, and slept on the way to and from Japan even though any city worth bombing was heavily guarded by anti-aircraft guns. Blood pressure (nervous in the service it was dubbed) was a problem for only a few. Only one member of the replacement group that I went from Langley Field, Virginia, to Guam with developed this condition. However the entire eleven-man crew of some B-29s "chickened out." Such crews would fly from their base in the Mariana Islands to a point over the Pacific Ocean not far from where they should cross the coastline of Japan and then drop their bombs into the Pacific.

My journey to Guam originated at Langley Field, Virginia. My training as Radar Observer, Bombardier/Navigator was completed there. When it was completed we were given the choice of war theaters—European or Eastern. My friend, Tom Marshall, was a Californian. He wanted me to see California—at least some of it. Those of us selecting California were put on a troop train and sent to Hamilton Field, San Rafael, California. From there we were sent, also by troop train, to Fort Lewis, Washington. At both ends of a railroad coach car, and on both sides, the rear seat back was fixed. On all other seats, the frame of the seat back was hinged to the floor so that when reaching the end of the rail line, it was unnecessary to turn the coach around. Only to flip the seat backs from the side they were onto the other.

While traveling between San Rafael and Seattle I was playing poker with three strangers—ignoring the standard advice: never play big money poker with strangers, and "You got to know when to hold 'em and know when to fold 'em, know when to walk away, and know when to run." We were playing five-card draw, nothing wild, table stakes (once the dealer picks up the deck to shuffle, no player can lay more money on the table). The individual opposite me dealt me a good hand to draw to. I found myself holding three eights. As was his right, the dealer had called for a game of draw. After the opening betting round was completed, the dealer, of course, called out the word, "cards." I tossed away my two odd cards and asked for two more. One of these was another eight. Four of a kind. Very rare. So I was sitting pretty. A skilled poker player and a heavy bettor sat to the immediate right of the individual sitting opposite me. I kept the betting alive and each time it was my turn I would raise. Heavy Bettor was not only hanging in, but also he, to my great pleasure, also raised at every opportunity. I stopped raising only after Heavy Bettor ran out of chips. Completing the betting, I stopped raising and called. Heavy Bettor showed a full house and reached out with both hands to pull in the chips. I stopped this by putting one hand firmly on his and threw my cards; face up, onto the table. When he saw my four of a kind, his face flushed. I could see that I was playing with what is known as a sore loser. It was my turn to deal. I dealt myself three sixes. When the opening betting was over and we had all pitched the cards we didn't want, I dealt to each player the number of cards that he had discarded, as usual. I dealt myself another six! The betting followed the pattern of the previous hand. Heavy Bettor had refreshed his money supply. Betting was getting heavy and the two other players dropped out. Heavy Bettor was eyeing my pile of cash thinking of it as his. He was dead set on getting it all back. He chucked in his whole wad. I called him.

So he also lost that wad and was sure that I was cheating. Red-faced mad, he decided to get his money back. He dived over the table at me. The table was a board about five feet wide and five or six feet long which we held on our laps. Cards and everyone's money went on the floor. The two innocent bystanders, sitting with us, went for the aisle. This pushed the Heavy Bettor into the aisle. He was fighting to get at me. They, and others nearby, tried to restrain him. There was instant chaos. The fighting in the aisle spread. It looked like a bar room brawl. One cadet was not fighting—I was on the floor picking up the money and stuffing it in my pockets. The troop commander, a colonel, came in, took a quick look, and turned off the car lights. Later, the lights came back on. Most of the gang was asleep. I stayed awake all night to keep an eye on Heavy Bettor. I wasn't born yesterday.

The train, heading north, stopped at a small town between San Rafael, California, and Fort Lewis, Washington. It was parked so that it blocked the main street of the town. Looking westward out of the coach window, I could see, the business section, three or four blocks away. Having sat there bathed in sweat for about an hour, I got up and announced that I was walking to the first restaurant for a cool drink or a cup of coffee. Three or four others joined me.

We sat at the counter enjoying our drinks. Every minute or two, one of us would step outside to see if the train conductor was waving his lantern and calling, "All aboard." One of our group stepped out, took a look and reported that the train was gone. The group, except for me, got up and ran for the door. They arrived at the same conclusion I'd arrived at—running after the train would produce nothing but sweat and shortness of breath. They came back to join me and finish their drinks. Seemed obvious that panic would not solve our problem.

Behind us, sitting in a booth, were two young men. One of them tapped me on the shoulder. He said that the train was headed north and that for many miles on this side of the track, the road went side-by-side with the tracks. "In a few spots," he said, "land contours take the train a short distance from the road." He offered us a ride saying that if we followed the road, sooner or later we would catch the train. We piled into his car and chased the train. Sure enough, in less than five miles, we saw the train parked at what turned out to be a siding—the line was a single track and our train was on a siding waiting for a southbound freight train to pass. We bailed out of the car and after a quick thanks climbed over a fence and ran. The conductor saw us and held the train until we were aboard. The remaining trip to Fort Lewis, Washington, was completed and we boarded a troop ship. The ship dropped our five-man group in Honolulu. From there we flew to Guam.

Prior to the time that I started flying missions to Japan the following incident happened. Early in the war bombing was accomplished by formation flying. At the time the bombardier of every plane in a group released its bomb load when the lead plane dropped its bombs, with the bombardier using the Norden bombsight. On one of the early missions the target was Kobe. My friend, Lucas, a pilot, flew this mission and as usual flew the lead plane in a large formation. His bombardier was named Boley. As Luke's plane approached Kobe and was over Kobe Bay, an anti-aircraft shell exploded in front of and close to the plane. Boley was bounced backward and accidentally toggled out the bombs. Of course the entire group toggled out. Many fish were killed in what we dubbed "the famous Kobe Bay drop." Boley was advised that his plan to starve the Japanese into submission was a brilliant strategic idea and that he had made a very important contribution to the war effort. Luke was an airplane commander. I flew several missions with him. Being a multi-engine pilot (what single-engine pilots called straight and level guys), Luke flew in what I call a conservative manner. We took turns flying—Luke flew one mission, I flew the next. Luke's landing procedure involved a slow rate of descent starting, maybe, a hundred miles from the airfield. Single-engine pilots stayed at flying altitude—could be 5,000-12,000 ft. where the air was smoother. Lower altitudes meant bumpy rides especially if the sun was up because of rising air currents. As a single-engine pilot approached a field for a landing he killed altitude quickly by cutting the throttle and making steeply banked turns up to 60 or 70 degrees right, left, etc. during the descent. Steep banking angles reduced lift and increased the rate of descent. Maximum wing lift is achieved only when the wings are horizontal, of course.

Returning to Guam on one occasion with Luke at the controls he started his usual slow rate of descent to landing altitude. Some of the crew members got on the intercom and asked him to give me the controls. They really enjoyed the roller coaster effect of the way I killed altitude. I was highly amused at his reaction. When it became necessary to lose altitude he simply pushed hard on the stick. I can still see the grim, determined look on his face while all crew members and everything loose in the plane, including the latrine in the rear section, hit the ceiling. Luke remained seated only because of his tight grip on the control stick. Luke was a gentleman and insisted on cleaning up the mess, but it never smelled the same back there. I was glad that I sat in the front section.

I was flying a mission with Captain Munger over Japan when we lost an engine. Orders were, in such an event, to forget the mission and fly to Iwo Jima, our emergency landing field and refueling station. During the war I had to land there six times. We immediately set a course for Iwo Jima. Between us and the coastline I looked for what was called a "target of opportunity." The only target was a small village through which ran railroad tracks which hugged the coastline from the southwestern tip of Japan to the northeastern tip. This village was maybe a hundred to a hundred and fifty miles south of Tokyo and not a suitable target. Just north of the town, maybe three or four miles away, the tracks disappeared into a tunnel. The tunnel was the only available target. So I instructed the bombardier to drop the bomb load on the tunnel entrance. This was actually "Operation Overkill." We had no choice and no illusions. The tunnel would not be out of operation very long. The railroad, as far as I could tell, was Tokyo's principal north-south lifeline, but better than no target at all—the province of the bombardier. Bomb detonators acted as a trigger does on a gun. Each bomb had a cotter pin in the business end of the bomb, which prevented accidental discharge. Just prior to a drop the bombardier removed the cotter pins. The cotter pin had a tag attached. I saved one tag on each mission and wrote on the tag target identity, type of bomb (demolition or napalm), drop altitude, and date. I still have these.

There was a blackout, as usual, in Tokyo on the nights of May 24, and 25, 1945. B-29s were conducting a "burn job" (dropping napalm bombs) on Tokyo. The city was 90 percent leveled. Viewed from above (I flew over Tokyo later returning from an "after the war" mission dropping supplies at a POW camp) one looked down at a grid of streets, sidewalks, and short sidewalks perpendicular to the streets leading to either squares or rectangles of black ash. Lost my best buddy, Tom Marshall, whose plane was shot down the first night. Although not scheduled, I volunteered for the second night to avenge Tom's loss. I later learned from the intelligence office that, in wiping out the Tokyo metropolitan area, we had seriously crippled necessary support of Japanese troops in the eastern war theater and that some 90,000 civilians had been killed. War is not pretty, but they started it. They had one more reason to regret the mistake they had made at Pearl Harbor.

The B-29 was designed for high-altitude bombing, 30-40,000 feet. This didn't work out. Bombing is always done flying upwind which lowers ground speed, thereby increasing accuracy. We learned for the first time that there was a jet stream having a velocity greater than the B-29s airspeed. When flying into the wind at that altitude, the planes on the first raid of the war against Japan actually found themselves going backward and away from Japan. After that discovery I do not remember flying above 12,000 feet. We flew one mission at 2,000 feet. Japanese kids, I said at the debriefing which followed each mission, were throwing pop bottles and shooting BB guns at us.

A B-29 had an eleven-man crew. The B-29 crew size was

as follows: in the front capsule, bombardier, airplane commander, pilot, navigator, engineer, and radioman. In the rear capsule were the central fire control gunner, left gunner, right gunner, and radar bombardier/navigator. The tail gunner was not in a capsule. For high-altitude bombing, it had two airtight capsules at the front and at the rear connected by a 32-foot tunnel running over the top of the bomb bay. There is no doubt that Japanese radar picked us up early in a mission. They always knew when we were coming, which planes were coming, where we were going, and the name of the airplane commander of each plane. When B-29s were within radio range we could receive Tokyo Rose on our radios. She played the '40s big band music (Glen Miller, Benny Goodman, Dorsey Brothers) and, using the names of some of the airplane commanders on that mission, would announce that they would not be returning. Tokyo Rose was wrong. The intent was to demoralize—it was pure propaganda. They returned to the Mariana Islands. One thing was for certain; she had the names right and knew that they were on the raid. The U.S. did not have a monopoly on spies and spying.

Whenever a plane did not return from a mission, and the officer crew members were quartered in the Quonset I was assigned to, I waited for three or four days hoping that they had ditched and been picked up by our Air/Sea Rescue Service. During this time, I kept an eye on their living area—a bunk and a cabinet—to ensure that nothing was stolen. If they did not appear after five days, I collected their valuables for safekeeping. If they were still missing after five weeks, I mailed valuables (money converted into a money order) to their home in the U.S. I waited five weeks thinking by that time they would have been notified that their loved one was missing in action. On one occasion I received a letter from alarmed parents. I was dismayed—obviously they had not been notified. I had to write them that their son was missing in action.

On another occasion, after a crew had not returned from a mission, an officer walked into our Quonset and, without announcing who he was, strode to the bunk area of Sydney Hoenig who was one of the crew members missing in action. We had been hoping to hear that he, and the rest of the crew, had been picked up by an Air/Sea Rescue team. At the time I was seated on my bunk about fifteen feet from Hoenig's area. The officer's back was to me as he started to go through Hoenig's possessions. I jumped up and started for him. Luke shouted a warning and the officer turned and saw me. He ran out of the back door and never returned. I searched Hoenig's area and collected his valuables. I found money under his mattress, rolled up in his socks, in his neatly folded underwear, in the tips of his shoes, and in books. I converted the money into a money order and sent it to his parents.

On the missions some crew members slept and some stayed awake. Missions ran from 12 to 18 hours. The two pilots could take turns at the controls and sleeping. Generally I read a book—I had taken many books to Guam. On one occasion I was flying with an Air Commander who was on his first mission. As we left Japan, he gave the navigator permission to sleep. I objected but was overruled. The navigator had given us a compass heading for Iwo Jima, which I knew from experience, was wrong. It would carry us about 35 miles west of Iwo.

The A/C, Adamson, was eight years younger than I, had a big ego, and had been hiding behind a door when brains were passed out. He had been flying in a manner, which increased the probability of us being shot down. At one point I forcefully knocked his hands off the controls and told him to keep them off. As we had left Japan he announced that this was his plane and took back the controls. He flew the heading given to him by the navigator. When the estimated time of arrival at Iwo arrived, Iwo was not in sight. He asked me if I knew where it was. I nodded in affirmation. He asked where Iwo was. I knew exactly where Iwo was and that we had missed it by roughly thirty-five miles. I also knew that islands are hard to spot from the air when the ocean has hundreds of shadows cast by cumulus clouds. It didn't help matters that our radio compass was not working.

Finally with Iwo forty or fifty miles behind and to the left of us, he swallowed his pride and radioed Iwo for a heading. He came to see me the next day and said, "If I hadn't called Iwo for a heading, you would have let us continue until we ran out of fuel and had to ditch, wouldn't you?" I said, "Yes, you had made it very clear that the plane was your plane." After a long pause he asked me if I would be his pilot for the rest of the war! Told him that, if he were the Air Commander of the last remaining plane in the world, I would not fly with him. From that time until the war was over, I could not get rid of him—he stuck to me like flypaper. He looked to me for advice about problems with his parents and his girlfriend.

A road paralleled the coastline from the North Field to and beyond Agana. At Agana, a side road ran uphill about half a mile to a banana plantation. A shortcut from my Quonset to the plantation could be made by walking through the jungle. Three airmen living in my Quonset and wanting bananas took the shortcut and were never heard of again—the jungle was alive with Japanese who had simply melted into the jungle when our marines took Guam. I drove a jeep to the plantation and asked the native plantation owner for bananas. He did not understand English, so I pointed at his banana field and he gave me a stalk of them. I asked him how much by rubbing a thumb and forefinger together and he threw up his hands for a "don't know" reply. I handed him a dollar and he was elated.

Immediately north of Agana between the road and the ocean was a good beach. It was about forty or fifty feet wide—ocean on one side, a row of tall cocoanut palm trees on the other. Agana also had a naval base and a naval hospital complete with nurses—the only white women on Guam. The nurses walked and sunbathed on the beach. It was a very popular place for off-duty aircrew personnel. One of the nurses often seen at the beach was very beautiful and had a great figure. When she strolled the beach, interest in watching the surf diminished to zero. One day I was sitting there with a friend as this nurse strolled by. "She's available for 200 dollars," he said. She was on Guam for six weeks and was transferred back to the U.S. A friend told me that she took $16,000 back with her—probably at least $200,000 in today's dollars. At that rate she was earning at a rate of $1,350,000/yearly. How she must have hated to go home.

Guam was a large reef which millions of years ago, by action of the deep underground plates, had been pushed up to the point where it was now a rugged, mountainous island roughly twelve miles long and, maybe three miles wide at the widest point. Roughly two miles square had been bulldozed to make North Field which had an elevation of 500 feet. This exposed a lot of lava and made it necessary to wear shoes or have your feet cut to ribbons.

Because of the heat and humidity I showered every evening. I accomplished this by leaving my Quonset attired in a helmet and shoes and carrying a bar of soap. I walked down the so-called road and peered into upended 55-gallon fuel drums which littered the area. These were devoid of fuel, but full of rainwater—it rained every evening. When I found one that appeared reasonably clean, I would shower by pouring water over my head, soaping up, and rinsing off. Also went to a movie most evenings, at the nearby 29th bomb group open-air theatre, so attired. The Japanese also enjoyed our movies. They remained in the jungle close to the theatre perimeter. Because of this, and because it was dark at movie time, I was more formally attired than when I showered. In addition to my helmet and shoes I wore my gun belt and holster. The .45 was in my hand—cocked and safety off.

After breakfast most mornings, I would, attired as above, find a shady spot in front of my Quonset and sit on my cot reading a book. At the time, Air Force officers could date navy nurses stationed at Agana only if they wore full uniform, drove a jeep, and carried the Colt .45 issued to all combat officers. The jungle was full of Japanese who simply melted into the jungle when the U.S. took the Marianas away from Japan. Mentioned my attire because nurses riding in jeeps driven by an airforce officer frequently drove by. They would give me a big smile and a wave. I figured that in their profession they had, no doubt, seen better.

Always feel sad when I think about Lieutenant Kepplar. She was a young, beautiful Navy nurse stationed at the navy hospital in Agana. She and my friend, Dick Jones, were in love. He was one of the four replacements who arrived with me at North Field. Dick had, prior to the war, lived with his parents in Minden, Nevada. He and Lt. Kepplar planned to marry as soon as they returned to the U.S. after duty on Guam. One morning, after visiting a friend who was quartered in a Quonset near a southeast corner of the airfield, I was walking back to my quarters going north and walking along the side of the road. Ahead of me, across the two runways, and maybe a mile away, I saw a plume of smoke. An airforce truck (ammunition carrier) came along going my way. I hailed it and asked for a ride to the source of the plume of smoke. I suspected the worst because Dick (a navigator) was scheduled to fly that morning. I wanted to check it out.

It was a plane wreck and a tangled mess. From the identifying letter and numbers, I saw that it was the plane in which Dick had been scheduled to fly that morning. My heart sank. An ambulance (meat wagons we called them) was parked nearby. I walked around to the other side of the wreckage, saw body bags and personnel searching the area for body parts. I asked about Dick—all service personnel wore on a chain about the neck, which carried a pair of "dog tags." These tags had imprinted on them the name and serial number of the bearer. One of the men pointed to a body bag. I asked if I could help with the search. They were grateful. I picked up such things as the toe of a shoe, which had been sheared behind the toe line of the shoe. Five toes dropped out. Ripped fuselage aluminum metal can be as sharp as a razor. I picked up an arm with a shoulder and lung attached. Finishing the search we left the area. I went straight to the mess hall. It was past my lunchtime and my appetite was intact. I'll never forget the military funeral for Dick. It was held at a cemetery on a hill overlooking Agana Harbor. The casket was flag draped. A marine squad stood at attention. An airforce chaplain spoke and read from the Bible. Lt. Kepplar was facing me from the other side of the casket. The squad fired a rifle salute. Lt. Kepplar was quietly sobbing. I wish I could erase that from my memory.

During the fourteen-to-eighteen-hour roundtrips Guam/Japan I read books (e.g., Gibbons, *Decline and Fall of the Roman Empire*) and slept. Things did not warm up until we got to Japan. I held the rating of airplane commander, pilot, and radar bombardier/navigator.

The airplane commander sat in the left, front seat (with

a crew of eleven he was a busy guy) and the pilot sitting in the right-front seat did much of the flying. After single engine training I held the rating of single engine pilot (trained in a P40). Volunteered for radar training hoping to fly P38s, which were equipped with radar. Picked up a Radar B/N (bombardier/navigator) rating. My first eleven missions were in that capacity. What the major didn't know was that I had never had my hands on B-29 controls, or for that matter, the controls of any multi-engine plane. It was a smooth, uneventful ride. I was given a rating of B-29 Pilot. Same thing happened again and I received the rating of airplane commander. Flew my remaining missions in the right-front seat as pilot. Thus, I am sure, I was the only B-29 pilot bombing Japan with zero multi-engine flying time. My flying time consisted of 650 single-engine hours. After the two atom bombs were dropped in mid-August, 1945, Japan surrendered and I flew just two more missions.

(1) Prisoner of war camp supplies. Supplies were strapped to a very heavy wooden pallet. The load weighing 3000–4000 pounds was attached to a large parachute. Three B-29s flew this mission. The camp was located inland at about the latitude of Tokyo. Dropping was difficult—the camp was located on the east side of a narrow winding north-south river valley near the south end of the valley. The valley was wider about 6–7 miles south of the camp. Deep cloud cover made descent a problem—we didn't know whether or not the cover extended to the ground. Using radar, we flew south to where our topographical map showed the valley was much wider. We circled down through the cloud cover hoping for visibility needed to fly up the valley. If the clouds extended to the ground, we could well crash because we could not adjust our altimeter to the local barometric pressure. In friendly territory this

would be accomplished by calling in to the nearest control tower and asking for the barometric pressure, which is needed to calibrate the altimeter.

Of the three planes assigned to the mission, one disappeared (crashed), one dropped the load onto a small village across the river from the camp killing the mayor and fifteen others (learned this from a later intelligence report). Our plane managed to drop the supply pallet in the camp but at a spot where no prisoners could be hurt.

(2) On September 5, 1945, General MacArthur and Japanese officials dressed in formal black suits and with top hats signed a peace treaty on the deck of the battleship *Missouri*, anchored in Tokyo Bay. I was flying one of the B-29s circling overhead in a show of strength formation.

For a short time, while on Guam, I was assigned to Mission Control, which meant control of the field and other duties. Prior to launching the raid, a single B-29 manned by a select crew flew to the city targeted by the raid. This plane dropped a fire (napalm bomb) at the center of the target area setting up the bull's eye. This was called "first strike" and immediately upon dropping their bombs they notified Mission Control by radio. When I received this message I would call General Powers to advise him. Earlier, maybe eleven o'clock, General Powers would come into the mission control center, tell me that he was going to bed, and ask me to call him when I heard from "first strike."

The mission controller also had control of the field. I had not been informed of this. I found out one dreary, rainy evening when, over the intercom, I had a call from the tower asking me whether or not the field was open. I hadn't been advised I had such power! I flipped the intercom to Weather and asked for flying conditions. I was advised; ceiling 2000 feet, visibility two miles. I was looking out of a nearby window as I told the weather officer, "Yes, I can see out of my window also." Such weather is okay but not the best for flying. I closed the field. About ten minutes later, the outside door of Mission Control burst open with a bang and an enraged, full colonel (also known as a bird colonel) confronted me. I knew what was wrong instantly. To have 50 percent added onto their monthly salaries, the last week of every month, "desk" pilots by hook or by crook squeezed in the required four hours of flying time. The colonel stood in front of my raised desk, raging, and forcefully made it known that he was a colonel and that I was a mere lieutenant. Major Moore who was in charge emerged from his office on the other side of the large mission control room, tapped the colonel on the shoulder and asked what the problem was. "I want to fly and this lieutenant has closed the field," said the colonel. Major Moore replied, "If the lieutenant closed the field, it is closed."

Japan being a country of Asia, is an archipelago of close to 143,000 square miles. For perspective, the U.S. has over 3 million square miles including Hawaii and Alaska. Japan is mountainous except for the east and west coastal plains coastline.

In the north/south mountainous region of mid-Japan and west of Tokyo is a river valley. The section of the valley immediately west of Tokyo is wide enough for a B-29 to spiral down into. Going north from the wide area, the valley becomes narrow and winding for ten to twelve miles. At that point the valley widens to about 1,000 yards for roughly a mile. Here, the valley abruptly ends with a sharp incline of about 2,000 feet. The POW camp was located on the east side of the river—on the west side was a small village.

The day was warm and humid, we were on a westerly heading as we approached Japan. Beneath us and as far as we could see in all directions, except behind us, was a cumulus cloud cover. With guidance from the radar observer, we spiraled down through the cloud cover reasoning that, because of the rising moist air over the river, visibility would be okay below the clouds. It was.

Going north toward the POW camp meant following the many turns of the river. We were boxed in: river below, cloud cover above, mountains on both sides. The valley was winding with many sharp bends. I was flying the plane. Never knew what would confront us as we cleared a bend. A waterfall or turn too sharp for a B-29 and we would crash. Some turns required banking the plane as much as 70 degrees. Multi-engine pilots consider anything over 16 degrees aerobatic. I planned the drop—the bombardier had no clue.

A drop coming from the south was not possible because of the winding river valley. A drop from the north was possible. The line of flight would be perpendicular to the fence line and rows of barracks. Due to low cloud cover, we had to fly at an altitude of about 250 feet.

The pallet parachute could not deploy because of the low altitude. If we dropped the pallet in the camp we would kill Americans. If we dropped the pallet outside the camp, the Japanese would get the goodies. I decided to toggle (a hand held switch which released the bomb bay load) out the pallet so it would not hit a barrack but would knock down the far fence line. Using our altitude and ground speed, and allowing for my reaction time, I calculated that I had to toggle out as we passed over the third row of barracks. It worked fine. After the drop we flew back to the camp. Prisoners were jumping up and down on the rooftops and waving American flags.

In the States, Chicken Shit was a very fair description for Adamson. The only person who liked Adamson was Adamson himself. There was no change on Guam. I had just walked past the command center Quonset hut at North Field when I heard a door slam open, footsteps running down the steps and in my direction, and a voice shouting "Eddie!" I turned around to see Adamson running towards me. I first met him while taking advanced flying training at Foster Field. Officers under his command disliked him. He gave me a big hug. That was in April or May of 1945. From that day until I left Guam in November, he clung to me like a leech.

One day he appeared and wanted advice (Adamson was an airplane commander. He sat in the left front seat; the pilot sat in the right). His pilot had refused to fly with him that day. Every member of the crew hated Adamson's guts. He said that he thought that he should report this to the command center and asked if I agreed. I told him that if he did there would be an investigation and every member of his crew would be questioned and he would end up peeling potatoes. To keep the matter under wraps, I flew as his pilot. That is why I have flown one more mission than is shown on my record.

We lived in Quonset huts. They were a half cylinder, curved side up, galvanized corrugated steel about twenty or twenty-two feet in diameter and, perhaps, sixty feet long with screened windows, and screened ends, each having a door. The wooden floor was twelve or fifteen inches off the ground. Jungle surrounded the field and both sides of the road leading to Agana. Many Japanese who had survived the battle for Guam hid in the jungle, and anything that was left out at night was stolen. Sentries had their throats cut. Shoes were the only things taken. The Japanese had no use for guns or money.

After the stop in Kwajalein, we flew to Hawaii and parked the plane overnight at Hickam Field. We stayed overnight at the bachelors' quarters—most large fields have one. I got out of my flying fatigues, showered, shaved and put on the standard officer's uniform. I went to the business (downtown) section of Honolulu and sat down at the soda fountain of the first drug store I came to. Across the counter in the worker's aisle, was a mirrored wall located just above the marbled shelf of a cupboard. On the top and inside of the cupboard, were cups, saucers, bowls, plates and supplies. I found myself immediately opposite a bunch of bananas. Fruit had been scarce in the Marianas. A bath towel would have been helpful for drool control. A waitress appeared and asked me what I wanted. I asked for a banana. She said that she couldn't do that. I said that I would pay for a banana split, but just wanted a banana. The manager appeared. He asked, "What's the problem?" The waitress explained. He took a quick glance at me, saw my air force officer's uniform (complete with Lieutenant's insignia, pilot's silver wings and various medals). The manager said to the waitress in a loud and angry voice, "Give the man a banana!"

Early in the War, we destroyed aircraft factories and other targets with 500, 1,000, or 2,000-pound demolition bombs. The Japanese were industrious and generally had the plants back in operation in a short time. So we demolished entire cities by burning them with napalm bombs. We demolished Tokyo on the nights of May 25 and 26, 1945. It was reported at the time that 90 percent of the city had been reduced to ashes. Once a city was burned out, it stayed that way until the war ended—no utilities, no stores, no public transportation. When a metropolitan area was burned out, many planes were involved. The idea was as you approached the city on the bomb run, you just picked out a spot that wasn't on fire and dropped bombs there. The heated air, of course, rose, thereby creating severe air turbulence, which made for a very bumpy plane ride. Actually, this tore the wings off planes from time to time. We saw planes go down, and we saw one plane back on Guam with the wings bent up at a 30-degree angle. Must have had dicey flying that one back to Guam.

Once I forgot to fasten my seat belt. We seldom belted up on a raid to reduce exit time in case we took a hit. On burn jobs a belt came in handy because the severe bouncing around made it difficult to control the plane. Our plane hit a downdraft and I found myself plastered on top of the fuselage. Then we caught an updraft and I found myself on the floor, squished between the seat, the rudder controls and the control stick. The bombardier had the same problem and was unable to toggle out the bombs. The airplane commander wanted to abort and return to Guam. I said that we were being paid to drop bombs and that we were not going to chicken out. He had very few missions under his belt but had enough sense to know at the debriefing he would look chicken. We made a second and successful pass.

Flight personnel arrived in the Eastern Theater of Operations one of two ways:

1. As a complete crew, trained in a B-29 in Wichita, Kansas, where B-29s were produced and arriving in the Pacific arena in the B-29 they trained in, or,
2. As crew member replacements. I arrived on Guam with four other individuals to replace individual losses. I had volunteered into the U.S. Army Airforce in Cleveland, where I worked at the time. I was an executive for a subsidiary of U.S. Steel when I volunteered. My thinking at the time was that, if I was not in the service, someone else was fighting the war for me.

I arrived at North Field, Guam, with four other crew members:

—Tom Marshall (Bakersfield, CA). Close friend. Shot down while on Tokyo raid.
—Dick Saleeby. Story follows. Lost in action.
—Dick Jones. Killed in airplane accident.
—Gene Mason. Lost it. My memory is not clear. He may have been returned to the U.S. as a Section 8 case. I was the only one leaving North Field as I arrived—alive and sane. I would not want to put this to a vote.

One dark night, and in very bad weather, I tuned our radio to Iwo (Ranger Tower) as we were passing by Iwo on our way to Japan. Heard a pilot and friend, talking to Ranger Control Tower. He had lost three engines; they were down to two thousand feet, were twenty miles from Iwo on a heading of 165 degrees from Ranger, and were bailing out. I called Ranger and asked if they could use our help. Ranger called back saying yes, and that a destroyer was on the way, but due to darkness and high seas, the destroyer would have little or no chance of success. I instructed the bombardier to salvo our bomb load into the Pacific and, for much needed altitude accuracy, called Ranger for the barometric pressure reading needed to fine tune our altimeter. Then dropped to 200 feet, flew a 165-degree course over Ranger Tower, and flew the 165-degree track by crossing the track, making a U-turn left crossing the 165-degree line, making a U-turn right, etc. The radar observer had no trouble keeping us on line. It was dangerous work—pitch black, stormy weather, and high seas. With only 200 feet between the water and us, and with high waves and a wing span of 141 feet,

I had to have a lot of trust in my instruments and my instrument flying capability. Sharp turns needed to keep a tight pattern would put the down wing to about sixty feet closer to the water. The waves were twenty feet, or more, and an instrument or flying error would have been fatal. I saw what I thought was a flashlight blinking. I told the radar operator to take a hack (heading and distance) from Iwo and told the radio operator to notify Ranger so that they could give this information to the destroyer. I kept in touch with the destroyer via Ranger. We could see the destroyer coming our way. After what seemed like forever, Ranger called to inform us that seven individuals had been picked up. Great news. Continued the search. Again saw what I thought was a blinking flashlight. Two more were located. We saved nine individuals, but my buddy, Saleeby was not among them. From my ocean charts I knew the direction and velocity of the ocean current at the area we were in. So, until our gas ran too low (well after daylight), we continued to search the area into which a raft, or individual in a life jacket, would drift because of the currents. No luck. Touched down at Iwo with the gas gauges bouncing near zero. I have often wondered: was Saleeby already dead or did he helplessly watch us search and not see him? Very hard to spot an individual in the ocean if there are waves of significant size. Mechanics at Iwo cleaned the plane. They said they had never seen, or cleaned, a plane covered with so much salt. Incidentally, one of the problems we had during the search had been the salt covered windshield.

During a daylight raid—can't remember which city—we took a hit just under the No. 2 engine nacelle which took out the engine and damaged the landing gear. Retracted wheels are located in the nacelles of No. 2 and No. 3 engines—immediately to the left and the right sides of the body of the plane. Hydraulic mechanism was damaged and we could not get the wheels down even with the hand crank. I had immediately hit the button needed to douse, or prevent, a fire in that nacelle.

With no landing gear we would have to belly-in when we arrived back at North Field, Guam. Upon arriving close to Guam, I told the engineer to dump all fuel into the Pacific except for enough to fly a normal landing pattern and land (this to minimize the possibility of fire or to reduce fire damage).

Then told the crew to throw everything, which was loose (including the Norden bombsight—not loose but which could, with a rough landing, break loose and become a dangerous flying missile) into the bomb bay. Also, ordered doors and windows, which with a rough landing could jam, detached and thrown into the bomb bay. This done, I told the bombardier to salvo the stuff into the Pacific.

Skidded 3,200 feet on the macadam runway which became a long, flat, grinding wheel. Ground off some of the bottoms of the front and back machine gun turrets and eight to twelve inches of the plane's belly. I will never forget the smoke and smell of the burning metal.

The name of the oldest living Japanese fighter pilot was Chicken Teriyaki. We were on a daylight raid and were over Japan when I saw a Japanese fighter (a Zero) coming at us at eleven o'clock high. Informed the gunners that we had a Zero at eleven o'clock high turning to make a pass. In a split second I heard our turrets open up. Immediately the Zero had a trail of smoke behind him and the pilot bailed out. Our central fire control gunner, I now knew, was one hell of a shot. Our gunners did not fire on the parachuting pilot—some B-29 gunners did. Our gunners thought that killing someone definitely taken out of action and dangling from a chute bordered on plain murder. I was pleased with their thinking.

Over Japan we took an anti-aircraft burst close and just

under the No. 2 nacelle. Really bounced us around. The anti-aircraft battery responsible got lucky. Our altitude, speed, the differences in the wind at that altitude (can't remember but we were probably between 6,000 and 12,000 feet) made a hit less a matter of skill than a matter of luck or statistical probability. The Japanese had many anti-aircraft batteries around Toyko, of course, and other important cities like Nagoya which was heavily industrialized. The hit we took was too close for comfort. Had it been any closer we would have lost the wing and gone down. I told the crew that after we landed, to keep them entertained on the way down, I would have played Taps for them on my kazoo. We had a fun crew—lots of kidding around. Once, on a very rocky night over Tokyo, one of the gunners punched his mike button and said, "Hey Ed, throw your book at them." I always had a book, or books, with me on the missions which lasted anywhere from twelve to eighteen hours.

The burst shut down that engine and damaged the landing gear (left wheel retracts into the left inboard engine nacelle; right wheel into the right inboard nacelle). This meant a belly landing on Guam. As we approached Guam I had the flight engineer salvo most of our fuel into the Pacific leaving enough for a landing but not much to spare. A belly landing on the asphalt runway would be like grinding off the bottom of the plane, and the fore and aft gun turrets, with a giant grinding wheel complete with burning metal, sparks, etc. Dumped excess fuel to reduce the amount of fuel available to start, or feed, a fire. Munger (airplane commander) sat in the left-front seat and I (pilot) sat in the right. Munger, who was a very good and experienced pilot, brought the plane in for a landing. I told him to make it good because I would not leave enough fuel for a go-around (second pass). From the point of touchdown, by actual measurement, we skidded 3,200 feet. As the plane leveled off for a landing I told the engineer to cut off all fuel switches (engines would suck all fuel from the lines thereby reducing the chance of a fire), pressed my mike button, and advised all hands that when the plane stopped skidding the last one out was an SOB. Fire, or worse an explosion, was my concern. As we skidded along the plane filled with white smoke and the smell of burning aluminum. When the plane stopped skidding we all left like corks out of a popgun, ran to the side of the runway, and dived over.

Years later I had a little grandson who liked to dress up in my Air Force fatigues, which were too big for him. One day he came stumbling in with a crumpled piece of paper, which he'd fished out of the pocket. "What's it say, Gramps?" he asked. It was written in Japanese. Not wanting to disappoint him, I dragged out of my memory:

Tom Marshall, Dick Saleeby, Dick Jones, Gene Mason, and the unknown name of that dead Japanese, whose pocket I had picked so long ago.

I put it together with a poem from my past.

Here, lie we dead
Because we did not choose
To shame the land from which we sprung.
Life is, perhaps, no great thing to lose
But young men think it is
And we were young.

And so was that Japanese.